行健CP依儀那尚賞：

弘揚陶瓷

後學

Jayoo Li

2023.1.6 美气

目錄

目錄

國立聯合大學 校長 序

　　近代著名的教育家蔡元培先生曾經指出，學生要養成「健全的人格」必須要從四方面進行教育，分別是體育、智育、德育、美育，他說：「美育者，與智育相輔而行，以圖德育之完成者也。」聯合大學創校之初以培育工業領域人才為主，隨著國家發展的人才需求，相繼成立六個學院：理工、電資、管理、客家研究、人文與社會、設計等學院，成為深化教學與務實研究並重的大學。在歷任校長卓越帶領及校內師生同仁共同努力下，校務發展蒸蒸日上，院系亮點及成果卓越，享有盛譽；此外，本校同時也重視學生的「美育」發展，校園內設置藝文中心，加以人文氣息和客家、原民文化的薰陶，人文藝術氣息濃郁，相信能為大家打造自然科技及人文藝術的優質校園，因此學生與校友在藝術方面成績斐然，時獲殊榮，為校爭光，全校師生與有榮焉，傑出校友李仁燿先生即是本校榮光。

　　李仁燿傑出校友於創作之餘，秉持著「施比受更有福」的信念，回饋社會，推廣陶藝美學，致力陶藝技術的傳承。曾在母校國立聯合大學兼任助理教授，將知識及技藝傳承予學弟妹。尤其難能可貴的是，長年定期於各級學校義務指導後輩學子，莘莘學子從李仁燿老師的「0.01公分小口瓶」體悟「有容乃大」的人生哲學，從小口瓶發現大大的宇宙乾坤。

　　李仁燿傑出校友目前已是享譽國際的陶藝大師，但他多年來不忘母校，知恩圖報，襄助母校發展，令人深受感動而肅然起敬！李仁燿傑出校友適逢母校於2022年創立50週年生日慶，慨然允諾再捐贈心血結晶的珍稀陶藝作品9件，合併前年所捐贈，總計50件以資校慶紀念，其中小口瓶30個、容器7個、蜂巢茶壺5支、茶碗3個、書法4幅及水墨畫1幅，回饋母校永久典藏，嘉惠母校師生，祝賀聯合50週年大慶。其贈與事蹟，增添校園藝文氣息，璀璨美育成果更精彩可期！

　　李仁燿傑出校友飲水思源，知恩反饋的美德，也正是聯合大學前進不懈最大的鼓舞與動力，本人謹在此代表本校師生同仁深表謝忱，今天藉由這本築夢《李仁燿老師陶藝專輯》的編撰，讓我們懷抱著感恩與歡欣的心情迎接聯合50，同時也祝福聯合大學校運昌隆，生日快樂！

國立聯合大學 校長 李偉賢 謹誌

Preface from the President

Tsai Yuan-Pei, the famous educator of the modern period, once pointed out that to cultivate the highest level of integrity in students, educators should simultaneously focus on four things - physical education, intellectual education, moral education and aesthetic education. He said, "Aesthetic education together with intellectual education leads to the success of moral education." Since its beginning, National United University (NUU) has emphasized the development of students' talents and their potential in the field of industry and technology. To meet the needs of national development, NUU then set up six colleges: the College of Science and Engineering, College of Electrical Engineering and Computer Science, College of Management, College of Hakka Studies, College of Humanities and Social Sciences, and College of Design. Since that time, NUU has been a comprehensive university emphasizing teaching and academic research equally. Under the excellent leadership of former presidents along with the contribution of teachers and students, NUU has thrived year after year and has become renowned for its departmental vigor and impressive individual achievements. In addition, NUU attaches importance to the development of students' aesthetic sense. With its strong humanistic ethos, and commitment to Hakka and aboriginal culture, NUU has created a superb milieu for the development of technology, the humanities, aesthetics and innovative art. Therefore, it can be said the current student body and alumni also have achieved their ambition to be crowned with the honor of recognition for their excellent performance. Li Jen-Yao, our outstanding alumnus, is one of the best examples.

In addition to creating art, Li Jen-Yao also believes that "giving is more blessed than receiving": giving back to society, promoting the aesthetics of the ceramic arts, and dedicating himself to the passing down of ceramic art technology. He at one point served as an assistant professor at his alma mater, National United University, passing on his knowledge and skills to the students coming after him. He has regularly guided the younger generation in schools at all levels for many years. His students acquire a philosophy of life, learning that "tolerance is great" as they discover the wide universe from the "small 100 micrometer bottle" of Mr. Li Jen-Yao.

Li Jen-Yao is now an internationally renowned pottery master, but he has never forgotten his alma mater despite the passage of many years. He always expresses gratitude for his alma mater and helps with its development. It is impressive and awe-inspiring! To celebrate the 50th anniversary of National United University in 2022, he promised to donate another nine rare ceramic works. Along with those donated two years ago, a total of 50 pieces will be exhibited to commemorate the school's anniversary. Thirty small-mouth bottles, seven containers, five beehive teapots, three tea bowls, four calligraphic pieces and one ink painting will make up his works in the school's permanent collection. The donation greatly contributes to the development of the artistic atmosphere and aesthetic education on campus.

Li Jen-Yao's example of gratitude is also the greatest inspiration and a driving force for innovation in aesthetics at NUU. On behalf of the faculty and current students of NUU, I would like to extend my sincerest thanks to Mr. Li. Let us celebrate with him the 50th anniversary of National United University with a sense of gratitude and joy, as we wish National United University a prosperous and happy birthday!

Woei-Shyan Lee, Ph.D., President of National United University

文化部 部長 序

　　臺灣擁有豐富多元的文化，在地理特色與歷史脈絡交織之下，地方文化得以孕育出獨特的生命力，也形塑涵養地方特色工藝發展。臺灣製陶的歷史由來已久，曾發展出包括鶯歌、苗栗、南投、嘉義、北投、美濃等陶業聚落，各自精彩，各具風華。

　　陶藝家李仁燿生於臺灣陶瓷重鎮之一的苗栗，自幼接觸在地陶藝文化的濡染，曾就讀於聯合工專陶業工程科（現為國立聯合大學材料科學工程學系）奠定陶藝創作基礎。他透過家鄉的陶土實踐對美的探索，舉凡人物、動物雕塑、造型現代陶雕、手捏生活陶及傳統手拉坯等等，展現多元的創作視野。其中，他多年來潛心鑽研的「小口瓶」獨特技藝最為人所知，以高超的技巧首創內徑最小0.01公分、僅能放入一根秀髮的小口瓶。小口瓶口小細頸、肚大而能藏乾坤，創作時尤須全神貫注，創作失敗率也相當高，其作品曾獲選為2012年「臺灣世界網球爭霸賽」冠軍獎盃，讓世界網壇知名的冠軍得主喬科維奇（Novak Djokovic）大為讚賞。

　　李仁燿以開創性的「小口瓶」創作挑戰自己的藝術巔峰，同時也演繹「有容乃大」的人生哲學。秉持著堅持不懈的工藝精神，創作不輟、不斷突破自我，加上熱衷於陶藝推廣與社會公益，2011年建國一百年獲頒全國十大傑出青年藝術文化獎的殊榮。為了回饋母校及社會，李仁燿曾在國立聯合大學兼任助理教授，並於各級學校、偏鄉學校授課，致力於陶藝教育及推廣。今年，欣逢國立聯合大學創校五十週年校慶，李仁燿作為傑出校友再次慨捐創作予校方典藏，加上2020年「蘊菁陶采－李仁燿陶藝創作30年經典巡迴個展第19站暨捐贈母校典藏」之捐贈數量，共計捐出50件作品，嘉惠母校師生之外，更希望讓陶藝之美傳承下去。

　　百尺竿頭更進一步，在精研陶藝三十多年之後，李仁燿先生今年考取國立臺灣大學資訊網路與多媒體研究所博士班，嘗試探究藝術與科技領域結合更多新的可能。他在藝術創作上的勇於創新與突破，在文化傳承推廣上的熱心參與，令人敬佩！值此創作專輯付梓之際，特綴數語，以表敬意與賀忱。未來，至盼其持續為臺灣陶藝發展開創新局，持續貢獻所長提攜後輩，為臺灣工藝界引入更多支持的力量。

文化部長 李永得

苗栗縣政府文化觀光局 局長序

來自大湖的李仁燿老師，長年以來投注在陶藝領域，並以小口瓶為代表作品，並於100年榮獲十大傑出青年藝術文化獎，是苗栗非常具有代表性的藝術工作者。從事陶藝創作之餘，也致力於推廣陶藝，傳承技藝，更曾擔任中華民國陶藝協會理事長、苗栗縣陶藝協會理事長等重要社團幹部，努力讓從事陶藝的創作者有更好的環境與交流平台。

然而，斐然成績的累積也並非毫無挫折；在2005年時，工作室不幸發生火災，讓長年努力的一切付之一炬，但李仁燿老師憑藉著堅強的意志力重新起步，鑽研手拉坏難度最高的小口瓶，並運用最適合燒製的苗栗土，創造出屬於自己的品牌與鮮明的辨識度；除了造型上的追求極致外，釉藥的運用也創造出繽紛絢爛的色彩，在質樸與華麗之間找到絕妙的平衡。

為了精益求精，更上層樓，今年李仁燿老師還考取了國立臺灣大學電機資訊學院資訊網路與多媒體研究所博士班（一般生），除了祝賀金榜題名，更是對孜孜不倦的求學精神感到由衷敬佩；除此之外，李仁燿老師也不忘本，不僅曾經擔任母校國立聯合大學的兼任助理教授，將所學傳授給學弟妹們，也在母校48週年與50週年生日時，慨然捐贈各類型藝術作品，累計共計50件精心創作，包含小口瓶、蜂巢茶壺、水墨畫、書法等，回饋母校永久典藏，湧泉相報之心令人動容。

今欣聞國立聯合大學50週年校慶，為感念李仁燿老師捐贈作品，特別出版專輯，謹誌一文表達恭賀之意，並期待未來李仁燿老師能在創作的道路上持續突破，為苗栗的陶藝寫下一頁頁輝煌的篇章。

苗栗縣政府文化觀光局 局長 林彥甫 謹誌

藝術中心 主任序

　　今年欣逢國立聯合大學創校50週年，即將於11月25日舉行校慶系列活動，這是值得慶賀的時刻，也是重要里程碑。回首過去，聯大一路走來披荊斬棘、步步維艱，從專科、學院到今日的「深化教學與務實研究並重之大學」，不論是硬體建設的展現，或是教學卓越、產學研發軟實力的深耕，皆屢創佳績，受到各界的肯定和鼓勵。

　　國立聯合大學迄今已邁向第50個里程碑，在文化的傳承與藝術的校園生活中，藉由本校藝術中心舉辦三場藝術展，包括10/3-10/28吳季如老師創作展、11/7-12/2「高原之美」張秋臺水彩畫展、以及預計於12月展出曾文忠老師西畫展，同時我們亦特別將校友李仁燿陶藝作品印製成作品集專書，一起為聯大慶生。

　　李仁燿今年52歲，出生於苗栗大湖農家，高中時期開始投入陶藝創作。2005年一場大火，導致經營十多年的工作室及陶藝作品付之一炬，但李仁燿並未因而懷憂喪志，他有如浴火重生般，開始研究手拉坯中難度最高的小口瓶，運用家鄉在地富含23%～26%鐵質的苗栗土，拉製燒造出瓶口內徑最小只有0.01公分、僅容髮絲通過的陶藝作品，開創了小口瓶的新天地。

　　孜孜矻矻努力多年，李仁燿獲得中華民國100年十大傑出青年藝術文化獎的殊榮，他的陶藝作品精緻出色，廣受各方好評與青睞，例如曾獲選為2012年「台灣世界網球爭霸賽」冠軍獎盃，當年冠軍得主喬科維奇大為讚賞。

　　李仁燿於創作之餘，秉持著「施比受更有福」的信念，回饋社會，推廣陶藝美學，致力陶藝技術的傳承。曾在母校國立聯合大學兼任助理教授。尤其難能可貴的是長年定時於各級學校義務指導後輩學子，莘莘學子從李仁燿老師的「0.01公分小口瓶」體悟「有容乃大」的人生哲學，從小口瓶發現大大的宇宙乾坤。

　　尤其令人敬佩的是，李仁燿精研陶藝三十多年之後，百尺竿頭更進一步，今年（111年）考取國立台灣大學電機資訊學院－資訊網路與多媒體研究所博士班（一般生），繼續研究藝術與科技的結合，更上一層樓，精益求精，足為在校學弟妹們的楷模。

　　這次得以順利印製成《李仁燿老師陶藝專輯》的築夢作品，謝謝許多幕後功臣的鼎力支持，謝謝本校李偉賢校長、秘書室李宜穆主秘、以及共同教育委員會張陳基主委，以及協助展場規劃與專書出版工作的黎冠宣先生，謝謝大家。

李志布 謹誌

李仁燿 自序

　　身為83級材料（陶業工程科）畢業生，能為國立聯合大學五十週年校慶之喜增添光彩，便是將個人多年在陶藝創作的努力成果回贈母校，以茲資彰顯並感謝當年的培育之恩。除為個人榮耀的分享，更多期望是藉此拋『陶』之舉得以引玉，啟發與鼓勵校友追求個人生命的熱情，在各行各業均得以實踐自己。

　　說到陶藝創作，這是我的一生追求，然每每回想緣起，往往總會覺得是發自小時候生活的體驗。從小出生於苗栗大湖農家，造就而後對於自然事物的觀察及體悟，能有更深刻的敏銳。加上從小因書法而對藝術產生濃厚興趣，高中時期開始投入陶藝創作，透過陶土探索美的領域。自1986年算起，我的陶瓷學習與創作過程，一直以來都為多元化樣貌呈現，不論是人物、動物、雕塑、造型現代陶雕、手捏生活陶以及傳統手拉坯等各種形式作品皆有。創作生涯中最重要的時刻，當為自2005年開始研究手拉坯中難度最高的小口瓶時期。選擇運用家鄉在地富含23%～26% 鐵質的苗栗土，以一氣呵成的精神與技法製出瓶口內徑最小只有0.01公分、僅容髮絲通過的雅致作品，不僅開創了小口瓶底天地，更以小口瓶共同建構了陶藝生命創作的新時代。曾有評論如此說道：『小口瓶樸實的外表卻有華麗的內在，簡單的線條卻有撥人心弦的悸動。口小肚大藏乾坤，圓潤的瓶身，裝滿富貴、智慧與圓滿，細小的瓶口，教導「厚積而薄發」、及「虛懷若谷」的處世之道』。曾經，小口瓶作品獲選作為2012年「台灣世界網球爭霸賽」的冠軍獎盃，讓當年冠軍得主喬科維奇為之驚艷。

　　今（2022）年幸逢母校建五十週年慶，特將創作的小口瓶、無極、容器、蜂巢茶壺、書畫等五大系列，總計50件作品捐贈母校、永久典藏、展示。作為台灣陶藝創作者一員，希望自己的作品能讓更多人欣賞到不同階段的創作，也驅動自己精益求精、持續創作更多元化的作品的同時，更想藉此吸引更多陶藝喜愛者積極參與創作、投入陶藝教育的傳承，因為台灣土也能做出世界級的陶藝品。

創作與教學過程中，個人仍深感所學不足，需要不斷的努力學習，繼2019年在母校國立聯合大學取得創新設計產業碩士學位後，今再於國立臺灣大學資訊網路與多媒體研究所博士班持續進修，希望從藝術與科技的結合，繼續不停的實驗，研究、創新、突破現狀，讓「精準小口瓶釉色」能夠透過新的理念與科技，未來能夠看到更璀璨的陶瓷大千世界。

李仁燿 學經歷

學 歷
1983 苗栗縣立武榮國民小學畢業
1986 苗栗縣立南湖國民中學畢業
1989 省立大甲高中美工科畢業
1996 國立聯合工商專校陶業工程科畢業
2000 朝陽科技大學工業設計系畢業
2019 國立聯合大學設計學院碩士畢業
2022 攻讀國立臺灣大學電機資訊學院資訊網路
     與多媒體研究所博士班（一般生）

經 歷
1986 榮獲苗栗縣國語文競賽中學組寫字第一名
1996 通過中華民國陶瓷－石膏模乙級技術士檢定
     第一位通過台中縣陶藝協會舉辦全國長年性
     拉坯檢定之永久免試資格
1997 擔任台中縣陶藝協會第一屆金陶盃捏陶比賽
     評審委員
     國立聯合技術學院陶藝社講師
2003 當選國立聯合大學校友總會監事
     國立聯合大學陶藝社講師
2004 榮膺苗栗縣社會優秀青年獎
     榮膺2004年全國十大傑出企業經理人
     美國聖地牙哥陶藝聯展
     國立聯合大學材料科學工程學系校友會會長
2005 受邀設計製作行政院客家委員會致贈入圍者
     獎牌
     第十六屆金曲獎紀念品（音符系列）
     第十四屆金鐘獎紀念品（經典系列）
2006 至法國巴黎藝術交流
     榮膺第六屆國家工商科技人才金像獎
     受邀設計製作行政院長致贈六雄傑出運動員
     獎牌（開花結果）
     受邀設計製作中華電信研究所外賓禮品
     （種子）
2007 榮膺中華民國第七屆傑出中小企業家金典獎
2008 榮獲台中市第十三屆大墩美展工藝類入選
     國立聯合大學材料科學工程學系校友會榮譽
     會長
2009 第四屆全球城市小姐選拔總決賽評審委員
     榮任苗栗縣陶藝協會第六屆理事長
2010 國立聯合大學客庄學院陶藝設計講師
     國立大甲高中美工科陶藝組講師～迄2018
     苗栗縣立南湖國中陶藝職群設計講師～
     迄2018
2011 榮膺中華民國第49屆十大傑出青年－藝術
     文化類
     獲日本國際公募藝術未來展入選

2012 美國伊利諾大學博物館永久典藏小口瓶作品
     「紅唇迷戀」
     獲選製作台灣世界網球爭霸賽冠軍獎盃
     連任中華民國陶藝協會第十一屆理事長
2013 榮任國立聯合大學課程諮詢委員
     中國北京大學永久典藏小口瓶作品「京
     鏵」、書法「真善美」
2014 榮任第七屆臺灣金陶獎陶藝競賽籌備委員
     中國北京大學永久典藏小口瓶作品「福韻
     京濤」
     榮任新竹縣文化局典藏委員
2015 榮任中華民國陶藝協會榮譽理事長
     中國哈爾濱工業大學永久典藏小口瓶作品
     「飛瀑丰姿」、書法「勤學」
     國際扶輪3500地區苗栗和平扶輪社第三屆
     社長
2016 榮任國立台灣工藝研究發展中心評審委員
2018 苗栗縣立開礦國小陶藝設計講師～迄今
2019 受邀國立國父紀念館逸仙藝廊舉辦「蘊菁陶
     采」李仁燿陶藝創作30年經典巡迴個展，揮
     毫45.5公尺書法，打破創館以來的新紀錄
2020 榮任文化部國際及兩岸文化資訊平臺諮詢
     顧問
     國立聯合大學工業設計學系兼任助理教授
     於台北忠孝店.中外藝品大賞及中壢SOGO遠
     東百貨「蘊菁陶采」李仁燿陶藝經典巡迴
     個展
     受邀母校國立聯合大學創校48週年校慶揮毫
     60公尺書法打破新的記錄
2022 立法院國會藝廊「蘊菁陶采李仁燿陶藝創作
     展」－邀請展
     考取國立臺灣大學電機資訊學院資訊網路與
     多媒體研究所博士班
     榮任長榮大學美術系外審專家委員

2012中華民國陶藝協會理事長李仁燿與世界網球球王喬科維奇

名稱：築夢
年份：2020
尺寸：32（高）*15（長）*15（寬）cm
材質／燒製方式：苗栗土，純手工拉坯完成，上志野釉加鈷紫色，再柴燒1250°C持溫22小時
說明：浪漫紫衣披上雅致的白紗，一身秀韻多姿，雍容華貴

（Artwork）Title：Building Dreams
（Artwork）Date：2020
Size：32（Height）*15（Length）*15（Width）cm
Medium/Materials：This Miaoli Clay masterpiece is finished with slip casting processed by hand, applied with
　　　　　　　　　Shino glaze with Cobalt violet color, then processed in a firewood kiln at 1250°C,
　　　　　　　　　fired for 22 hours.
Descriptions：This masterpiece expresses "A romantic purple dress coated with an elegant white veil is beautiful,
　　　　　　　colorful, graceful, and elegant."

名稱：飛翔系列-仰望
年份：2017
尺寸：19（高）*16（長）*16（寬）㎝
材質／燒製方式：苗栗土，純手工拉坯完成，用瓦斯窯燒1236˚C持溫3小時
說明：天高地闊，藍天白雲，我仰頭凝神靜觀，且待羽翼豐滿，將乘風飛去

（Artwork）Title：Flying（series）- Gazing
（Artwork）Date：2017
Size：19（Height）*16（Length）*16（Width）cm
Medium/Materials：This Miaoli Clay masterpiece is finished with slip casting processed by hand;
      This masterpiece is processed in agas kiln at 1236˚C, fired for 3 hours.
Descriptions：This masterpiece expresses the blue sky with white clouds. Imagine yourself looking up and gazing
      at the sky, and imagine your wings are fully spread, awaiting to soar in the wind.

名稱：瓜瓞綿綿
年份：2020
尺寸：23（高）*19（長）*19（寬）cm
材質/燒製方式：苗栗土，純手工拉坯完成，上綠色條紋釉，用瓦斯窯燒1239˚C
　　　　　　　　再降到1158˚C持溫5小時
說明：我盡最大的心意，在藤上結出滿滿的瓜，祝頌您昌盛不絕

（Artwork）Title：Prosperity
（Artwork）Date：2020
Size：23（Height）*19（Length）*19（Width）cm
Medium/Materials：This Miaoli Clay masterpiece is finished with slip casting processed by hand. This masterpiece
　　　　　　　　was applied with green glaze in a striped pattern and processed in a gas kiln at 1239˚C, then at
　　　　　　　　1158˚C, fired for 5 hours.
Descriptions：This masterpiece expresses. "I will do my utmost to bear melons on the vine to wish you
　　　　　　　prosperity."

名稱：窈窕
年份：2020
尺寸：28（高）*25（長）*25（寬）cm
材質/燒製方式：苗栗土，純手工拉坯完成，上鐵紅釉，用瓦斯窯燒1239˚C再降到1158˚C
　　　　　　　持溫5小時
說明：穠纖合度，玲瓏有緻，並光耀動人，恰似位窈窕佳人

（Artwork）Title：Graceful
（Artwork）Date：2020
Size：28（Height）*25（Length）*25（Width）cm
Medium/Materials：This Miaoli Clay masterpiece is finished with slip casting processed by hand, applied with
　　　　　　　　　ceramic red crystalline glazes processed in a gas kiln at 1239˚C, then at 1158˚C, fired for 5 hours.
Descriptions：This masterpiece expresses "Superbly detailed, exquisite and shining, just like a fair and beautiful woman."

名稱：深秋
年份：2020
尺寸：23（高）*20（長）*20（寬）cm
材質／燒製方式：苗栗土，純手工拉坯完成，用電窯燒1228°C持溫45分鐘
說明：紅似火的霞光，耀眼奪目，剎那即是永恆

（Artwork）Title：Late Autumn
（Artwork）Date：2020
Size：23（Height）*20（Length）*20（Width）cm
Medium/Materials：This Miaoli Clay masterpiece is finished with slip casting processed by hand,
processed in an electric kiln 1228°C, fired for 45 mins.
Descriptions：This masterpiece's fire-like red haze is dazzling. This masterpiece expresses the moment of eternal.

名稱：飛翔系列－全家福
年份：2017
尺寸：23（高）*24（長）*24（寬）cm
材質／燒製方式：苗栗土，純手工拉坯完成，再雕型上釉後，用瓦斯窯燒1233°C持溫2小時
說明：渾厚的身軀，豐實的羽絨，我羽翼下的全家福

（Artwork）Title：Soaring（series）- Family Portrait
（Artwork）Date：2017
Size：23（Height）*24（Length）*24（Width）cm
Medium/Materials：This Miaoli Clay masterpiece is finished with slip casting, then shaped and processed
by hand, and applied with glaze. Processed in agas kiln at 1233°C, fired for 2 hours.
Descriptions：This masterpiece expresses an abundant and rich plumage; This masterpiece expresses the family under
the head of the house's protection.

名稱：薪火韻永（薪火流傳）
年份：2021
尺寸：31（高）*16（長）*16（寬）cm
材質／燒製方式：苗栗土，純手工手拉坯完成，柴燒1250°C持溫16小時
說明：柴與火的融合，薪火代代相傳，永不止息

（Artwork）Title：Burning Fires（Passing down）
（Artwork）Date：2021
Size：31（Height）*16（Length）*16（Width）cm
Medium/Materials：This Miaoli Clay masterpiece is finished with slip casting processed by hand, processed in
a firewood kiln at 1250°C, and fired for 16 hours.
Descriptions：This masterpiece expresses, "The fusion of firewood and fire, the fire that passes from generation to
generation, never ends."

名稱：膽瓶－碧海擎天
年份：2020
尺寸：29.5（高）*16（長）*16（寬）cm
材質／燒製方式：苗栗土加瓷土，純手工拉坯完成，用瓦斯窯燒1239˚C再降到1158˚C持溫5小時
說明：貴氣的寶藍，在流金的陪襯烘托下，擎天而立

（Artwork）Title：bravery bottle/vase-Standing firm in the blue sky.
（Artwork）Date：2020
Size：29.5（Height）*16（Length）*16（Width）cm
Medium/Materials：This Miaoli Clay masterpiece is finished with slip casting processed by hand; This
　　　　　　　　　masterpiece is processed in agas kiln at 1239˚C then at 1158˚C, fired for 5 hours.
Descriptions：This masterpiece's "Aristocratic sapphire blue" color expresses the backdrop of gold
　　　　　　　outshines in the sky.

名稱：福祿
年份：2009
尺寸：24（高）*20（長）*20（寬）cm
材質／燒製方式：苗栗土，純手工拉坏完成，上綠釉，用瓦斯窯燒1235°C持溫2小時30分
說明：寬容的大肚，圓融的處世，福祿自來

（Artwork）Title：Happiness and Reward（Zebra stripes）
（Artwork）Date：2009
Size：24（Height）*20（Length）*20（Width）cm
Medium/Materials：This Miaoli Clay masterpiece is finished with slip casting processed by hand. This masterpiece
　　　　　　　is applied with green glaze and processed in a gas kiln at 1235°C, fired for 2 hours 30 mins.
Descriptions：This masterpiece expresses，"Happiness and prosperity will surely come with a generous stomach and a
　　　　　　balanced approach to the world."

名稱：梅瓶－天目流彩
年份：2017
尺寸：28（高）*16（長）*16（寬）cm
材質／燒製方式：苗栗土，純手工拉坯完成，上天目釉，瓦斯窯燒1236˚C持溫3小時
說明：黝黑的亮彩，流動的光影，尊貴天成

（Artwork）Title：Plum Vase-Teikoku psychedelia
（Artwork）Date：2017
Size：28（Height）*16（Length）*16（Width）cm
Medium/Materials：This Miaoli Clay masterpiece is finished with slip casting processed by hand and applied
                 with Tenmoku glaze in agas kiln at 1236˚C, fired for 3 hours.
Descriptions：This masterpiece's glossy dark shades, flowing brightness, and shadows express the masterpiece's
             moral nature.

名稱：花系列－菊君子
年份：2020
尺寸：22（高）*20（長）*20（寬）cm
材質/燒製方式：苗栗土，純手工拉坯完成，刻畫後柴燒1230˚C持溫24小時
說明：菊，花之君子。我以菊裝飾一身，剎時成了一位謙謙君子

(Artwork) Title ：Floral Series-Chrysanthemum
(Artwork) Date ：2020
Size ：22（Height）*20（Length）*20（Width）cm
Medium/Materials ：This Miaoli Clay masterpiece is finished with slip casting processed by hand.Engraved
　　　　　　　　with the pattern and processed in a firewood kiln at 1230˚C, fired for 24 hours.
Descriptions ：This masterpiece expresses "Chrysanthemum is the gentleman of flowers. This masterpiece's body is
　　　　　　　decorated with chrysanthemums, and immediately transforms into a modest gentleman."

名稱：耦合
年份：2017
尺寸：19（高）*15（長）*15（寬）cm
材質／燒製方式：苗栗土，純手工拉坯完成，用瓦斯窯燒1233˚C持溫3小時
說明：就這麼，我們依存在一起，你亮彩照人，我素樸沉靜，我們不分彼此

（Artwork）Title：Coupling
（Artwork）Date：2017
Size：19（Height）*15（Length）*15（Width）cm
Medium/Materials：This Miaoli Clay masterpiece is finished with slip casting processed by hand.
This masterpiece is processed in a gas kiln at 1233˚C, fired for 3 hours.
Descriptions：This masterpiece express, "So, we coexist together, you shine brightly, I, myself is simple and quiet,"
we do not distinguish each other.

名稱：觀音瓶系列－寶藍條紋瓶
年份：2020
尺寸：13（高）＊7.5（長）＊7.5（寬）cm
材質／燒製方式：苗栗土，上藍色條紋釉，電窯燒1228°C持溫2小時
說明：觀音寶瓶楊枝淨水，普降甘霖

(Artwork) Title：Bodhisattva vase series-Aqua marina striped vase
(Artwork) Date：2020
Size：13（Height）＊7.5（Length）＊7.5（Width）cm
Medium/Materials：Miaoli Clay, applied with indigo glaze with stripes patterns, processed in an electric kiln
　　　　　　　　at 1228°C fired for 2 hours.
Descriptions：This masterpiece expresses Bodhisattva Holding a Vase of Longevity (Kalasa), blessing the world and
　　　　　　　the land during the drought with rain.

名稱：金色年華
年份：2009
尺寸：25（高）*18（長）*18（寬）cm
材質/燒製方式：苗栗土，純手工拉坯完成，刻畫素燒後上褐灰釉，瓦斯窯燒1250°C持溫2小時
說明：無可取代的風華歲月，器物有情，鏤刻下我們昔日的榮光

（Artwork）Title：Golden Years
（Artwork）Date：2009
Size：25（Height）*18（Length）*18（Width）cm
Medium/Materials：This Miaoli Clay masterpiece is finished with slip casting processed by hand. This
　　　　　　　　　masterpiece is applied with graphite color glaze after engraving the design pattern,
　　　　　　　　　processed in a gas kiln at 1250°C, and fired for 2 hours.
Descriptions：This masterpiece expresses an "Irreplaceable years of glory, objects of love, chased our former glory."

名稱：鐵膽柔情
年份：2020
尺寸：21（高）*20（長）*20（寬）cm
材質/燒製方式：苗栗土，純手工拉坯完成，用瓦斯窯燒1239°C持溫5小時
說明：別看我一身粗曠，我用圓弧細緻的線條，展現我最柔美的樣態

（Artwork）Title：Tender toughness
（Artwork）Date：2020
Size：21（Height）*20（Length）*20（Width）cm
Medium/Materials： This Miaoli Clay masterpiece is finished with the slip casting processed by hand;
　　　　　　　　This masterpiece is processed in the gas kiln at 1239°C, soaking for 5 hours.
Descriptions： This masterpiece expresses "Don't look at me as a rugged vessel. I use rounded and delicate lines to
　　　　　　　show my softest and most beautiful attitude."

名稱：含光
年份：2022
尺寸：22（高）*19（長）*19（寬）cm
材質／燒製方式：苗栗土，純手工手拉坯完成，瓦斯窯燒1258°C持溫6小時
說明：葫蘆瓶，寓意吉祥福氣。釉彩意象：幽深靜謐中含著亮光，暖暖內含光

（Artwork）Title：Light Concealing
（Artwork）Date：2022
Size：22（Height）*19（Length）*19（Width）cm
Medium/Materials：This Miaoli Clay masterpiece is finished with slip casting processed by hand,
processed in agas kiln at 1258°C, and fired for 6 hours.
Descriptions：Pot of gourd shape to metaphor lucky and blessing. Glaze colors imaging: concealed ambiguous light
shining through the darkness and quietness.

名稱：靜夜
年份：2016
尺寸：30（高）*20（長）*20（寬）cm
材質／燒製方式：苗栗土，純手工拉坯完成，上寶藍色釉，用電窯燒1228˚C持溫2小時
說明：如墨的夜色，深邃的天空，將思緒帶向無盡的思念

（Artwork）Title：Tranquil Dusk
（Artwork）Date：2016
Size：30（Height）*20（Length）*20（Width）cm
Medium/Materials：This Miaoli Clay masterpiece is finished with slip casting processed by hand, applied with
　　　　　　　　　 Aqua Marina color glaze, and processed in an electric kiln at 1228˚C, fired for 2 hours.
Descriptions：This masterpiece expresses, "The night dark as ink, the deep sky, brings endless thoughts."

名稱：木干鳥棲
年份：2015
尺寸：46（高）*19（長）*19（寬）cm
材質／燒製方式：苗栗土，純手工拉坯完成，在刻畫鳥的意象，以柴燒1250°C持溫6小時完成
說明：眾鳥高棲，相濡以沫，一生的摯友

（Artwork）Title：birds sitting on a dry wood
（Artwork）Date：2015
Size：46（Height）*19（Length）*19（Width）cm
Medium/Materials：This Miaoli Clay masterpiece is finished with slip casting processed by hand. This masterpiece is
　　　　　　　　engraved with the image of a bird and was finished in a firewood kiln at 1250°C, fired for 6 hours.
Descriptions：This masterpiece expresses high-perched birds in the air helping each other; This masterpiece expresses
　　　　　　"together, we are friends for life."

名稱：雀屏
年份：2017
尺寸：16（高）*14.5（長）*14.5（寬）cm
材質/燒製方式：苗栗土，上寶藍結晶釉，瓦斯窯燒1235°C持溫1小時45分
說明：屏開金孔雀

（Artwork）Title：You are the one
（Artwork）Date：2017
Size：16（Height）*14.5（Length）*14.5（Width）cm
Medium/Materials：Miaoli Clay was applied with Aqua Marina color glaze,processed in a gas kiln at 1235°C,
　　　　　　　　　fired for 1 hour 45 mins.
Descriptions：This masterpiece expresses "A Beautiful Peacock Opening its Feathers Display in Nature."

名稱：守拙
年份：2019
尺寸：24（高）*19（長）*19（寬）cm
材質／燒製方式：苗栗土，純手工拉坯完成，再柴燒1230˚C持溫15小時
說明：沒有多餘的修飾，沒有不足的遺憾，我呈現最真的自我

（Artwork）Title：Stay Foolish
（Artwork）Date：2019
Size：24（Height）*19（Length）*19（Width）cm
Medium/Materials：With Miaoli soil, finished by pure hand throwing, and burned with wood to 1230˚C and maintaining the temperature up to 15 hours.
Descriptions：No extra decoration, and no the regret of insufficient, just presenting the true myself.

名稱：幽
年份：2020
尺寸：8（高）*9.5（長）*9.5（寬）cm
材質/燒製方式：苗栗土，上志野釉，柴燒1260˚C持溫26小時
說明：深遠寧靜

（Artwork）Title：Phantom
（Artwork）Date：2020
Size：8（Height）*9.5（Length）*9.5（Width）cm
Medium/Materials：Miaoli Clay, applied with Shino glaze. Process in a firewood kiln at 1260˚C fired for 26 hours.
Descriptions：This masterpiece express "Deep and tranquil."

名稱：孔雀開屏
年份：2020
尺寸：31（高）*18（長）*18（寬）cm
材質／燒製方式：苗栗土，純手工拉坏完成，上紫色加寶藍結晶釉，用瓦斯窯燒1239°C
　　　　　　　　再降到1158°C持溫5小時
說明：我不隨意展示我的美，而今，我已張開美麗的羽翼，等待您的佇足凝視

（Artwork）Title：Peacock "train-rattling"
（Artwork）Date：2020
Size：31（Height）*18（Length）*18（Width）cm
Medium/Materials：This Miaoli Clay masterpiece is finished with slip casting processed by hand and applied with
　　　　　　　　violet with Aqua Marina color glaze in a gas kiln at 1239°C, then at 1158°C, fired for 5 hours.
Descriptions：This masterpiece expresses, "I do not show my beauty freely, but now I have spread my beautiful
　　　　　　　wings and wait for you to gaze at me."

名稱：大破大立
年份：2019
尺寸：31（高）*18（長）*19（寬）cm
材質/燒製方式：苗栗土，純手工拉坯完成，柴燒1260°C持溫26小時
說明：掙脫既定的框架，突破傳統的思維，破繭而出，再造風華

（Artwork）Title：Divergent
（Artwork）Date：2019
Size：31（Height）*18（Length）*19（Width）cm
Medium/Materials：This Miaoli Clay masterpiece is finished with the slip casting processed by hand. Finishing the process in the firewood kiln at 1260°C soaking 26 hours.
Descriptions：This masterpiece expresses "breaking through from the established framework, the traditional thinking, re-create a new style, emerging from the cocoon."

名稱：飛來一筆
年份：2016
尺寸：22（高）*18（長）*18（寬）cm
材質／燒製方式：苗栗土，純手工拉坯完成，至南投柴燒1235°C持溫12小時
說明：似乎是多餘，卻又似巧合，我們成就了一個特殊

（Artwork）Title：Astone
（Artwork）Date：2016
Size：22（Height）*18（Length）*18（Width）cm
Medium/Materials：This Miaoli Clay masterpiece is finished with slip casting processed by hand. Process in a firewood kiln in Nantou at 1235°C fired for 12 hours.
Descriptions：This masterpiece expresses, "Seemingly superfluous, yet seemingly coincidental, we have achieved something special."

名稱：花系列－心口
年份：2020
尺寸：24（高）*22（長）*22（寬）cm
材質／燒製方式：苗栗土，純手工拉坯完成，刻畫素燒後上志野釉加鈷紫釉，柴燒1250°C持溫22小時
說明：是刻意，是有心，一個出口，讓彼此情意流動，看似殘缺，卻見圓滿

（Artwork）Title：Floral Series-Heart Core
（Artwork）Date：2020
Size：24（Height）*22（Length）*22（Width）cm
Medium/Materials：This Miaoli Clay masterpiece is finished with slip casting processed by hand, applied with Shino glaze with Cobalt violet glaze after engraving with design patterns, processed in a firewood kiln at 1250°C, fired for 22 hours.
Descriptions：This masterpiece express "A deliberate, intentional, outlet for the flow of mutual affection," which is seemingly broken, but see the perfection.

名稱：順應
年份：2008
尺寸：31（高）＊16（長）＊16（寬）cm
材質/燒製方式：用苗栗土純手工拉坏完成，排窯時作品躺著用柴燒1256°C持溫12小時，
　　　　　　　呈現圓形土塊三個點的柔美變化
說明：接納自己的不足，隨順世緣，清靜無為，大智慧也

(Artwork) Title ： Obedience
(Artwork) Date ： 2008
Size ： 31（Height）＊16（Length）＊16（Width）cm
Medium/Materials ： This Miaoli Clay masterpiece is finished with slip casting processed by hand; The masterpiece
　　　　　　　is fired at 1256°C for 12 hours, lying in the kiln, presenting the soft transition of the three points
　　　　　　　of the round clay.
Descriptions ： This masterpiece expresses, "Great wisdom is to accept one's shortcomings, follow the world, and be
　　　　　　　quiet and free of action."

名稱：突破
年份：2008
尺寸：21（高）*19（長）*19（寬）cm
材質/燒製方式：苗栗土手拉坯，瓦斯窯燒1236˚C持溫2小時
說明：作品意象的啟迪：形象臻於完美，卻仍有突破的可能，仍有喜出望外的結局

（Artwork）Title：Breakthrough
（Artwork）Date：2008
Size：21（Height）*19（Length）*19（Width）cm
Medium/Materials：This Miaoli Clay masterpiece is finished with slip casting processed by hand;
This masterpiece is processed in a gas kiln at 1236˚C, fired for 2 hours.
Descriptions：This masterpiece expresses the inspiring imagery: a perfect image, but still a breakthrough
of joy.

名稱：極限
年份：2013
尺寸：30（高）*22（長）*22（寬）cm
材質／燒製方式：苗栗土，純手工拉坯完成，柴燒八天七夜1235˚C持溫22小時
說明：再沒有任何困難可以擊垮我了…，我以最大的毅力與耐力，成就了現在的我

（Artwork）Title：Extreme
（Artwork）Date：2013
Size：30（Height）*22（Length）*22（Width）cm
Medium/Materials：This Miaoli Clay masterpiece is finished with slip casting processed by hand,
　　　　　　　　 processed in a firewood kiln for eight days and seven nights at 1235˚C, firedfor 22 hours.
Descriptions：No any difficulty can strike me down…with the maximum forbearance and patience, I achieved
　　　　　　 what I am now.

名稱：緊緊相依
年份：2018
尺寸：15（高）*30（長）*20（寬）cm
材質／燒製方式：苗栗土，純手工拉坯完成，柴燒1235°C持溫16小時
說明：燒製過程底部爆裂而粘在坯體上呈現另一種美，注定一輩子要在一起，長相廝守，
　　　請你用厚實的背膀，帶我走一生

（Artwork）Title：Two hearts
（Artwork）Date：2018
Size：15（Height）*30（Length）*20（Width）cm
Medium/Materials：This Miaoli Clay masterpiece is finished with slip casting processed by hand, processed in a
　　　　　　　　firewood kiln at 1235°C, and fired for 16 hours.
Descriptions：During the firing process, the bottom bursts stick to the blank, presenting the masterpiece with another
　　　　　　aesthetic side. This masterpiece expresses two lovers destined to be together for the rest of their lives,
　　　　　　until death do them part.

名稱：花系列–出水芙蓉
年份：2020
尺寸：19.5（高）*19（長）*19（寬）cm
材質/燒製方式：苗栗土，純手工拉坏完成，刻畫花朵後素燒完成上志野釉，柴燒1250˚C持溫22小時
說明：我不嫵媚，不嬌麗，以清雅高潔的姿態綻放，風韻天成

（Artwork）Title：Floral Series - Hibiscus
（Artwork）Date：2020
Size：19.5（Height）*19（Length）*19（Width）cm
Medium/Materials：This Miaoli Clay masterpiece is finished with slip casting processed by hand. Applied with Shino glaze after engraving the flower patterns, and processed in a firewood kiln at 1250˚C, fired for 22 hours.
Descriptions： This masterpiece express, "I am not charming, not dainty. But I present myself with the elegant and noble attitude of blossom."

名稱：和合
年份：2021
尺寸：17（高）*22（長）*19（寬）cm
材質/燒製方式：苗栗土，純手工手拉坯完成，瓦斯窯燒1258°C持溫6小時
說明：含容大與小，端正與傾斜～高溫窯燒，器型變換出的和合相容，有驚喜有啟迪

（Artwork）Title：Harmony
（Artwork）Date：2021
Size：17（Height）*22（Length）*19（Width）cm
Medium/Materials：This Miaoli Clay masterpiece is finished with slip casting processed by hand in a gas kiln
　　　　　　　at 1258°C, fired for 6 hours.
Descriptions：Containing big and small, upright and tilting ~ kiln burning with high temperature so that the vessel
　　　　　　　transformed with adding and combining compatibility with amazing and inspiriting.

名稱：花器－扁瓶
年份：2015
尺寸：20.5（高）*20.5（長）*20.5（寬）cm
材質/燒製方式：苗栗土，純手工拉坏完成，用瓦斯窯燒1236°C持溫45分鐘
說明：扁瓶是常用花器，鎏金的色彩、渾圓的身軀，搭配各式花材，總能吸引觀眾的目光

（Artwork）Title：Floral Vessel-Flat Vase
（Artwork）Date：2015
Size：20.5（Height）*20.5（Length）*20.5（Width）cm
Medium/Materials：This Miaoli Clay masterpiece is finished with slip casting processed by hand; This masterpiece
　　　　　　　　is processed in a gas kiln at 1236°C, fired for 45 mins.
Descriptions：The flat vase is a commonly used floral vessel with a golden color and round body, which can always
　　　　　　　attract the audience's attention when matched with various floral materials.

名稱：花器－火印梅瓶
年份：2020
尺寸：28（高）*26（長）*26（寬）cm
材質/燒製方式：苗栗土，純手工拉坯完成，柴燒1230°C持溫24小時
說明：梅瓶是常見的花器，插上幾支梅花，禪意自現

（Artwork）Title：Floral Vessel-Firemark Plum Vase
（Artwork）Date：2020
Size：28（Height）*26（Length）*26（Width）cm
Medium/Materials：This Miaoli Clay masterpiece is finished with slip casting processed by hand in a firewood
　　　　　　　　　kiln at 1230°C, fired for 24 hours.
Descriptions：The Chinese Plum vase is a standard floral vessel with a few plum blossoms. This masterpiece expresses
　　　　　　　the concept of "Zen."

名稱：茶情柴韻（或：柴情彩韻）
年份：2021
尺寸：6（高）*16（長）*16（寬）cm
材質/燒製方式：苗栗土，純手工手拉坯完成，柴燒1236°C持溫3小時
說明：「茶」與「柴」音近似。此器型似茶器似花器，可觀賞可使用。高溫柴燒自然幻化的璀璨多彩

（Artwork）Title：Tea and firewood (Firewood Harmony)
（Artwork）Date：2021
Size：6（Height）*16（Length）*16（Width）cm
Medium/Materials：This Miaoli Clay masterpiece is finished with slip casting processed by hand in a firewood kiln at 1236°C, fired for 3 hours.
Descriptions："Tea" and "firewood" are homophonic puns in the Chinese language. The shape of this vessel is like a tea vessel or a flower vessel, and this pottery can be used for ornamental purposes. The high-temperature wood-fired vessel is naturally brilliant and colorful.

名稱：鐵紅結晶茶碗
年份：2018
尺寸：6（高）*11.5（長）*11.5（寬）cm
材質／燒製方式：苗栗土，純手工拉坯完成，用電窯1228˚C持溫3小時
說明：點點紅彩，似鐵鏽，又像是寬闊草原中恣意開放的繁花

（Artwork）Title：ceramic red crystalline glazes teacup
（Artwork）Date：2018
Size：6（Height）*11.5（Length）*11.5（Width）cm
Medium/Materials：This Miaoli Clay masterpiece is finished with slip casting processed by hand, processed in
an electric kiln at 1228˚C, and fired for 3 hours.
Descriptions：The dots of red color in this masterpiece resemble rust but also resemble the flowers opening freely in
the vast grassland.

名稱：虛心
年份：2020
尺寸：11（高）*20（長）*20（寬）cm
材質/燒製方式：苗栗土，純手工拉坯完成，刻畫素燒後上志野釉，柴燒1260°C持溫26小時
說明：虛其心，以容天下之物；虛其心，以納天下之美善

（Artwork）Title：Modesty
（Artwork）Date：2020
Size：11（Height）*20（Length）*20（Width）cm
Medium/Materials：This Miaoli Clay masterpiece is finished with slip casting processed by hand, applied with Shino glaze after engraving the design pattern, processed in a firewood kiln at 1260°C fired for 26 hours.
Descriptions：This masterpiece expresses "I have a humble heart to accommodate all the things in the world; I have a humble heart to accept all the goodness in the world."

名稱：土木親和
年份：2019
尺寸：21（高）*19（長）*19（寬）cm
材質／燒製方式：苗栗土，純手工手拉坯完成，柴燒窯燒1258°C持溫17小時
說明：人親土親，家鄉苗栗土的柴燒淬煉，成就此渾然天成質樸典雅的作品

（Artwork）Title：Connection
（Artwork）Date：2019
Size：21（Height）*19（Length）*19（Width）cm
Medium/Materials：This Miaoli Clay masterpiece is finished with slip casting processed by hand in a firewood kiln
　　　　　　　　at 1258°C, fired for 17 hours.
Descriptions：This masterpiece expresses the deep relationship with the land. Using Miaoli soil and processed in
　　　　　　　wood-fired refinement has resulted in this elegant work of natural simplicity.

名稱：寶藍條紋釉茶碗
年份：2020
尺寸：7.5（高）*12（長）*12（寬）cm
材質／燒製方式：苗栗土，純手工拉坯完成，上寶藍條紋釉用瓦斯窯1233°C持溫2小時
說明：優雅自適，在悠閒的午後與您相知相惜

（Artwork）Title：Aqua marina striped glaze tea bowl
（Artwork）Date：2020
Size：7.5（Height）*12（Length）*12（Width）cm
Medium/Materials：This Miaoli Clay masterpiece is finished with slip casting processed by hand. Applied with Aqua Marina color glaze process in a gas kiln at 1233°C fired for 2 hours.
Descriptions：This masterpiece expresses "Elegance and comfort, and an appreciation to get to know each other on a leisurely afternoon."

名稱：花器－寬口盆
年份：2016
尺寸：12（高）*25（長）*25（寬）cm
材質／燒製方式：苗栗土，純手工拉坏完成，上褐色釉，用瓦斯窯燒1235°C持溫1小時45分
說明：肚大能容，笑口常開，樸拙大器

（Artwork）Title：Floral Vessel-Wide Mouth Basin
（Artwork）Date：2016
Size：12（Height）*25（Length）*25（Width）cm
Medium/Materials：This Miaoli Clay masterpiece is finished with slip casting processed by hand and applied with brown glaze in a gas kiln at 1235°C, fired for 1 hour 45 mins.
Descriptions：The large vase "belly" accommodates a big smile; This masterpiece expresses "simple and humble."

名稱：三元素
年份：2018
尺寸：21（高）*20（長）*20（寬）cm
材質/燒製方式：苗栗土手拉坯，柴燒1236°C持溫2小時
說明：平衡的三元素創意，寓意天地人的和諧；紅色光燦的釉彩，寄寓平安吉利福氣

（Artwork）Title：Three Elements
（Artwork）Date：2018
Size：21（Height）*20（Length）*20（Width）cm
Medium/Materials：This Miaoli Clay masterpiece is finished with slip casting processed by hand in a firewood kiln at 1236°C, burned for 2 hours.
Descriptions：Creativity of balancing among the three elements, to metaphor the harmony of heaven, earth and human being; the glaze color of bright red signifying peace, lucky and blessing.

名稱：飛翔系列2-鷹眼（苗栗窯修建後第一窯的作品）
年份：2018
尺寸：9（高）＊15（長）＊10（寬）cm
材質／燒製方式：苗栗土，純手工拉坏再雕塑，最後用柴燒1250°C持溫16小時
說明：粗獷的泥塑，銳利的鷹眼，大氣自顯

（Artwork）Title：Soaring Series 2-Eagle's Eye (the first kiln after the construction of Miaoli kiln)
（Artwork）Date：2018
Size：9（Height）＊15（Length）＊10（Width）cm
Medium/Materials：This Miaoli Clay masterpiece is finished with slip casting and then shaping processed by hand. Finishing the process in a firewood kiln at 1250°C fired 16 hours.
Descriptions：This masterpiece is a rough and bold clay sculpture with a sharp eagle's eye, expressing that the atmosphere is self-evident.

名稱：經典
年份：2017
尺寸：9（高）*15（長）*10（寬）cm
材質／燒製方式：苗栗土，純手工拉坯完成，用電窯1228°C持溫2小時
說明：典雅古樸的造型，享受一壺清香

（Artwork）Title：Classic
（Artwork）Date：2017
Size：9（Height）*15（Length）*10（Width）cm
Medium/Materials：This Miaoli Clay masterpiece is finished with slip casting processed by hand. Finishing the process in an electric kiln at 1228°C fired for 2 hours.
Descriptions：This masterpiece expresses an "elegant" and "simple" shape.

名稱：韻味－金寶系列
年份：2020
尺寸：8.5（高）*15（長）*9（寬）cm
材質/燒製方式：苗栗土，純手工拉坏完成，用柴燒1250˚C持溫26小時
說明：元寶形狀的壺蓋鈕，吸納福氣、招財進寶

（Artwork）Title：Charm-Gem Ball Series
（Artwork）Date：2020
Size：8.5（Height）*15（Length）*9（Width）cm
Medium/Materials：This Miaoli Clay masterpiece is finished with slip casting processed by hand. Finishing the process in a firewood kiln at 1250˚C fired for 26 hours.
Descriptions：The Sycee-button-shaped lid is designed to invoke good fortune and attract wealth.

名稱：飛翔系列3-雙羽
年份：2021
尺寸：9（高）*14（長）*10（寬）cm
材質/燒製方式：苗栗土，手拉坯，瓦斯窯燒1236˚C持溫6小時
說明：來自和平鴿的靈感。愛惜羽翼，飛得高遠；萬里鵬飛，實現理想

（Artwork）Title：Soaring Series 3-Dual Feather
（Artwork）Date：2021
Size：9（Height）*14（Length）*10（Width）cm
Medium/Materials：This Miaoli Clay masterpiece is finished with slip casting processed by hand in a gas kiln at 1236˚C, fired for 6 hours.
Descriptions：Inspired from the peace dove which cherishes its feathers and flies far and high, to tens of thousands miles to fulfill the ideal.

名稱：融化－金寶系列
年份：2022
尺寸：9（高）*15（長）*9（寬）cm
材質／燒製方式：苗栗土，手拉坯，瓦斯窯燒1258°C持溫6小時
說明：器型平穩，線條流暢，釉彩典雅而散發出含蓄幽微的亮光，此壺有如好茶之韻味無窮

（Artwork）Title：Melted-Gem Ball Series
（Artwork）Date：2022
Size：9（Height）*15（Length）*9（Width）cm
Medium/Materials：This Miaoli Clay masterpiece is finished with slip casting processed by hand; This masterpiece is processed in a gas kiln at 1258°C, fired for 6 hours.
Descriptions：A smooth and stable vessel with smooth lines and an elegant glaze that emits a subtle and interval glow, this pot is like a good tea with an endless flavor.

書畫系列

名稱：愛陶
年份：2016
尺寸：180（長）*97（寬）cm
類別：書法

（Artwork）Title：Pottery Love
（Artwork）Date：2016
Size：180（Length）*97（Width）cm
Category：Calligraphy

書畫系列

名稱：超越
年份：2020
尺寸：180（長）*98（寬）cm
類別：書法

（Artwork）Title：Exceed
（Artwork）Date：2020
Size：180（Length）*98（Width）cm
Category：Calligraphy

書畫系列

名稱：禪
年份：2020
尺寸：180（長）*98（寬）cm
類別：書法

（Artwork）Title：Zen
（Artwork）Date：2020
Size：180（Length）*98（Width）cm
Category：Calligraphy

名稱：茶香
年份：2020
尺寸：158（長）*85（寬）cm
類別：書法

（Artwork）Title：Decoction
（Artwork）Date：2020
Size：158（Length）*85（Width）cm
Category：Calligraphy

名稱：雨讀勤耕
年份：2015
尺寸：130（長）*104（寬）cm
類別：水彩
說明：雨讀勤耕，怡然自得

（Artwork）Title：LOHAS
（Artwork）Date：2015
Size：130（Length）*104（Width）cm
Category：Watercolor
Descriptions：This masterpiece celebrates LOHAS（Lifestyles of Health and Sustainability）.

國家圖書館出版品預行編目(CIP)資料

國立聯合大學50週年校慶 : 築夢 : 傑出校友李仁燿
捐贈陶藝專輯 = National United University 50th
anniversary : forging dreams : distinguished
alumnus Li Ren Yao pottery album (donation)
/ 李宜穆主編. -- 初版. --
苗栗市 : 國立聯合大學, 2022.12
　面；　公分
ISBN 978-626-95423-6-9(精裝)

1.CST: 陶瓷工藝 2.CST: 書法 3.CST: 作品集
938　　　　　　　　　　　　　　　　111021000

書　　　名：國立聯合大學50週年校慶－築夢－傑出校友李仁燿捐贈陶藝專輯
英文書名：National United University 50th Anniversary－Forging
　　　　　Dreams－Distinguished alumnus LI REN YAO pottery Album
　　　　　(Donation)
發行單位：國立聯合大學
發 行 人：李偉賢
主辦單位：國立聯合大學藝術中心
協辦單位：國立聯合大學校友會、秘書室、共同教育委員會
編輯顧問：張陳基、李志成、黎冠宣
主　　編：李宜穆
編輯委員：潘玲玲、林淑珠、胡參琦、李仁燿
企劃編輯：黃勝銘
封面書法題字：李仁燿
印　　刷：原晟企業社
攝　　影：胡參琦
出版日期：2022年12月

ISBN 978-626-95423-6-9
版　　次：初版
定　　價：新臺幣300元
出 版 者：國立聯合大學
發行地址：36063苗栗市南勢里聯大2號
電　　話：037-382156
網　　址：https://art.nuu.edu.tw/
行政助理：劉清玉